SCIENCE ACTIVITIES

OUR ENVIRONMENT

VOLUME 7

John Bassett

GROLIER
EDUCATIONAL

Published 2002 by Grolier Educational
Sherman Turnpike,
Danbury, Connecticut 06816

FOR BROWN PARTWORKS

Project editor:	Lisa Magloff
Deputy editor:	Jane Scarsbrook
Text editors:	Caroline Beattie, Chris Cooper, Lesley Campbell-Wright
Designer:	Joan Curtis, Alison Gardener
Picture researcher:	Liz Clachan
Illustrations:	Darren Awuah, Mark Walker
Index:	Kay Ollerenshaw
Design manager:	Lynne Ross
Production manager:	Matt Weyland
Editorial director:	Anne O'Daly
Managing editor:	Bridget Giles
Consultant:	Victoria J. Cormie, MSc University of Leicester

Printed and bound in Hong Kong

Set ISBN 0-7172-5608-1
Volume ISBN 0-7172-5615-4

Library of Congress Cataloging-in-Publication Data
Science Activities / Grolier Educational
      p. cm.
      Includes index.
      Contents: v.1. Electricity and magnetism—v.2. Everyday Chemistry—v.3. Force and motion—v.4. Heat and energy—v.5. Inside matter—v.6. Light and color—v.7. Our Environment—v.8. Sound and hearing—v.9. Using materials—v.10. Weather and climate.
ISBN 0-7172-5608-1 (set : alk.paper)—ISBN 0-7172-5609-X (v.1 : alk. paper)—
ISBN 0-7172-5610-3 (v.2 : alk. paper)—ISBN 0-7172-5611-1 (v.3 : alk. paper)—ISBN
0-7172-5612-X (v.4 : alk. paper)—ISBN 0-7172-5613-8 (v.5 : alk. paper)—ISBN
0-7172-5614- 6 (v.6 : alk. paper)—ISBN 0-7172-5615-4 (v.7 : alk. paper)—ISBN
0-7172-5616-2 (v.8 : alk. paper)—ISBN 0-7172-5617-0 (v.9 : alk. paper)—ISBN
0-7172-5618-9 (v.10 : alk. paper)
      1. Science—Study and teaching—Activity programs—Juvenile literature. [1. Science—Experiments. 2. Experiments] I. Grolier Educational (Firm)

LB1585.S335 2002
507.1'2—dc21

2001040519

ABOUT THIS SET

Science Activities gives children a chance to explore fascinating topics from the world of science using the same methods that professional scientists use to solve problems. This set introduces young scientists to the scientific method by focusing on the importance of planning experiments, conducting them in a rigorous fashion so that a fair test can be carried out, recording all the stages, and organizing and analyzing the data to draw conclusions. Readers will have the chance to conduct exciting and innovative hands-on activities and to learn how to record and analyze their experiments and results in a variety of ways.

Every volume of *Science Activities* contains 10 step-by-step experiments, along with follow-up activities that encourage readers to find out more about the subject. The activities are explained and enhanced with detailed introductory and analysis sections. Colorful photos illustrate each activity, and every book is packed full of pictures and illustrations explaining the details of each topic.

By working fun and educational experiments into the context of the scientific method, anyone using this set can get a feel for how professional scientists go about their work. Most importantly, just have fun!

PICTURE CREDITS
(b=bottom; t=top)

Bio-Photo Services, Inc: 49 Kerry Dressler; **Corbis:** Lester V. Bergman 5, Becky and Jay Dickman 17, Ecoscene 31, Robert Estell 61 (t), Gallo Images 57, Gallo Images/Nigel J. Dennis 17, Mark Gibson front cover, Chinch Gryniewicz 26, Peter Johnson 55 (t), 61 (b), Bob Krist 37, Danny Lehman 21 (b), Gunter Marx 43 (t), Charles O,Rear 27, James Randklev 38, Arthur Rothstein 11, Kevin Schafer 23, Phil Schmeister 32, Premium Stock 12, Penny Tweedle 43 (b), Kennan Ward 4, Michael S. Yamashita 55 (b); **Ecoscene:** Angela Hampton 33, Sally Morgan 51; **Image Bank:** Harald Sund 6; **NASA:** 13, 21, 22; **Science Photo Library:** Martin Bond 56; **Still Pictures:** Philippe Bayle 39, Mark Edwards 13, 44.

CONTENTS

VOLUME 7
OUR ENVIRONMENT

INTRODUCTION

If you sprinkle seeds on the grass in your garden, birds will come and eat them and other plants. Cats come to eat the birds and scare away the mice. Your dog chases the cats. Tiny seeds have changed the ecology of your garden.

Our world contains millions of different living things, ranging from giant sequoias to insects, invisible bacteria, and viruses. All living organisms affect other organisms in some way. Ecology is the study of how organisms exist together and live in the world around them.

The place where an organism lives is called its environment. The environment includes everything that surrounds the organism, such as other organisms, the physical place where it lives, water, sunlight, air, and the climate. Some environments are very sensitive to change. If one small change occurs, it can have a major effect on all its organisms. If the environment changes too much, then some organisms in it may start to die out.

Earth itself is one large and sensitive environment. Changes in one part of the world can lead to the death of organisms in another. The destruction of one type of environment can lead to damage in other environments. Many environments are changing due to the action of one of the most destructive species on Earth—humans.

This book examines ecology. Ecology is the study of living organisms and how they fit into their environment. This book will also examine how we are damaging the world and how we can

◧ *The African veldt has a huge range of organisms, and they all affect each other. For example, plants grow after rain, gazelles come to eat them, and lions hunt gazelles.*

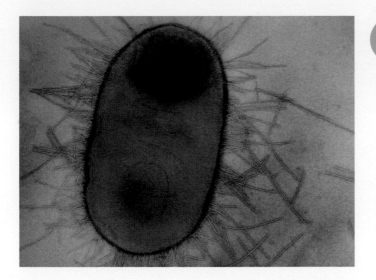

■ *This bacterium, called* **Escherichia coli (E. coli),** *lives in the human intestine. E. coli produces vitamin K, which is essential for helping blood clot.*

help reduce the damage. The activities in this book will show you how to collect information about your environment. In contrast, environmental scientists often collect data from very large areas. Every one of these areas may be made up of many smaller environments, each with its own landscapes, organisms, and weather conditions.

It is important to know that every living thing has a role to play in the environment. You may not like spiders because of the way they move, think earthworms are slimy, or dislike flies because they feed on waste; but without each of these creatures many others would die out, and the balance of nature would be destroyed. For this reason, whenever you are carrying out experiments that involve any type of animal, no matter how small, you must always treat the animal with respect. If you take anything out of the ground, then return it afterward. If you turn over a rock to see what lives underneath, then carefully put it back.

Some of the damage done to the environment occurs as a result of pollution. Much air pollution results from burning fuels. Garbage and toxic chemical waste, improperly disposed of, can contaminate land. This book will also examine some of the causes of pollution and contamination, possible solutions to the problems they can cause, and possible ways of reducing these problems.

The good science guide

Science is not only a collection of facts—it is the process that scientists use to gather information. Follow this good science guide to get the most out of each experiment.

● Carry out each experiment more than once. This prevents accidental mistakes skewing the results. The more times you carry out an experiment, the easier it will be to see if your results are accurate.

● Decide how you will write down your results. You can use a variety of different methods, such as descriptions, diagrams, tables, charts, and graphs. Choose the methods that will make your results easy to read and understand.

● Be sure to write your results down as you are doing the experiment. If one of the results seems very different from the others, it could be because of a problem with the experiment that you should fix immediately.

● Drawing a graph of your results can be very useful because it helps fill in the gaps in your experiment. Imagine, for example, that you plot time along the bottom of the graph and temperature up the side. If you measure the temperature ten times, you can put the results on the graph as dots. Use a ruler to draw a straight line through all the dots. You can now estimate what happened in between each dot, or measurement, by picking any point along the line and reading the time and temperature for that point from the sides of the graph.

● Learn from your mistakes. Some of the most exciting findings in science came from an unexpected result. If your results do not tally with your predictions, try to find out why.

● You should always be careful when carrying out or preparing any experiment, whether it is dangerous or not. Make sure you know the safety rules before you start working.

● Never begin an experiment until you have talked to an adult about what you are going to do.

ACTIVITY 1
A HOME OF THEIR OWN

If you live in a city, you could easily think there are no living things except people and their pets. But on any patch of ground, under any stone, or in any tree there is some form of life—worms, bacteria, beetles, and other bugs.

Every living thing, or organism, lives in a particular place. For example, polar bears live only in the Arctic—they cannot survive anywhere else. The type of place in which an organism lives is called its habitat. Almost everywhere on Earth is a habitat for some animal or plant. Habitats range from huge wild areas such as plains and rain forests to small corners of cities and yards, such as gardens and trashcans. A habitat can be as large as the tundra or as small as the soil in the pot of a houseplant. There are even organisms, such as certain types of bacteria, whose habitat is inside your body.

The soil in your yard or garden may not look as if it is teeming with life, but it is a habitat for many different organisms. Frost, rain, winds, and temperature changes break down rocks to make small mineral particles. These particles become soil. Every organism contains nutrients that can be used by other living things after the organism's death. When an organism dies, it is broken down into separate substances by other living organisms, such as bacteria or fungi. Some plants and animals, called decomposers, break down dead organisms and return their nutrients to the soil.

The materials produced when the organisms break down combine with minerals to form a rich soil called humus. It also contains water and air trapped between the particles. Millions of tiny creatures have their habitat in the soil, along with larger animals, such as worms and insects.

COMMUNITIES

Usually, many kinds of organisms live side by side in any habitat. To survive, they must all have food to eat. If there are too many organisms in a habitat, food will become scarce. But the numbers of one

🛡 *A rich ecosystem designed by a human being. The French painter Claude Monet created this garden around 1900. Fish, insects, birds, flowers, trees, and water plants live together in and around this pool.*

Ecosystem

A freshwater lake, its wildlife, and plants make up a complex ecosystem. The system depends on energy and resources that constantly flow into it. They include sunlight, fresh water from streams and rain, and oxygen from the air. Water evaporates from the lake, and gases are given out, including carbon dioxide and methane. In and around the lake there are many plant and animal populations, each consisting of individuals of particular species. The populations together make up the ecosystem's wildlife community. Within the ecosystem there are many different habitats: for example, reeds make a habitat for many species, while other species flourish on the lake bottom or at the water surface.

water plant habitat

ecosystem

individual

population

community

kind of organism are usually controlled by other living creatures that eat them. Where the habitats of organisms overlap, and different kinds of creatures exist together, they are described as a community. There may be only a few types of different organisms in a community or thousands. The community will almost always include both predators and their prey.

A community of organisms, together with the physical area that the community occupies, makes up an ecosystem. A pond and its wildlife make up an ecosystem; so does a rotting log that is teeming with microorganisms, insects, and fungi. Sunlight and any sources of water, like rain or rivers, are also part of an ecosystem. Ecosystems range in size from a small lake to a continent.

All the ecosystems that share a similar region and climate can be grouped together into a biome. Tropical rain forests are one example of a biome; all the grasslands of the temperate zone are another. All the biomes put together form the biosphere—the entire system of life and environment on Earth.

In the activity on the next pages you will look at the first stage in this series of interlinked systems by building a habitat for earthworms and examining the role they play in the larger ecosystem.

Earthworm Habitat

Goals

1. **Create a miniature earthworm habitat.**
2. **Observe the interactions of organisms and environment in the habitat.**

What you will need:

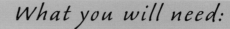

- clear container, such as a fishbowl or a plastic cup
- gravel
- sand
- potting soil
- compost
- chopped-up plant material
- straw
- spray bottle filled with water
- earthworms
- black paper
- tape

1 Into the container place a layer of gravel 1 inch (2.5cm) deep. Top with ½ inch (1cm) of potting soil, then 1 inch (2.5cm) of sand, 1 inch (2.5cm) of compost, and another ½ inch (1cm) of sand.

2 Top with chopped-up leaves, straw, and dead plant material.

3 Spray each layer with the water bottle as you put it in.

Handy hints

Remember to keep the contents of the bowl moist. If you are using a large bowl, then you can house more than one earthworm. Dig the earthworms out of your garden, or buy them at most pet stores. Remember, worms are living creatures, and you should try not to hurt them in any way.

4 Place the earthworms on top of the material in the container.

5 Cut out a circle of black paper to fit over the top of the container. Tape it in place, and make pinholes in the lid to allow air in.

6 Watch the worm habitat over the next few days. Make notes about the effects of the worm's movements.

How worms move

An earthworm moves through the soil by expanding and contracting its muscles. To move forward, it pulls its body together at the front and relaxes it farther back, which stretches the back part of its body. As the earthworm moves through the ground, it feeds by taking in soil through its mouth and filtering out the nutrients that it needs before discarding the waste from its back end.

7 Each day remove the lid, and spray the contents with water to keep them moist. After a week empty the habitat into your garden, a park, or other suitable outdoor area.

FOLLOW-UP (Earthworm habitat)

As the worm moves through the different layers of material in the container, you will notice two things happening. The first is that it will leave a clearly visible trail showing where it has been. The other is that the layers of soil will become mixed up. As the worm moves through the soil, it lets air into the soil layers. This air helps bacteria and other decomposers break down the dead material in and on the soil. The longer the worm stays in the soil, the more of the dead matter will decompose, turning it into rich compost for the soil. The worm also helps the process by eating the soil and vegetable matter and then passing it out.

Worms are not the only small organisms in the soil. To find out about others, carry out the following experiment.

What you will need:
large, clear container as in
    previous experiment
funnel
lamp
soil
gauze
magnifying glass

1 Place the funnel in the neck of the container. Drape the gauze over the funnel.

2 Put the soil on top of the gauze. Position the lamp so that it shines directly down onto the gauze, and turn on the lamp. Leave overnight. The light and heat will force the creatures that live in the soil down through the gauze and into the container.

3 Use a magnifying glass to look at the creatures that you find the following morning. Record the different types of animals in the container. If you do not know their names, draw them, and then look them up in reference books. Count the legs, wings, and body sections on each creature. This information will help you identify them.

Return all the animals and the soil to the same place that you took them from. You can then repeat this experiment using soil samples from different places around your neighborhood and draw up a map showing all the information you have gathered. You will get an idea of how many different creatures live in different types of soil.

ANALYSIS
A home of their own

Even though earthworms are small, they play a valuable role in the health of the biosphere. After watching them in their miniature habitat for a week or so, you may have figured out what this role is. Earthworms help distribute nutrients evenly throughout the soil. They do this in two ways.

As worms push their way through the soil, they mix up the different layers of the soil with their movements. In your experiment their movements were revealed by the trails they left as they moved through the miniature habitat. Earthworms also eat decaying matter near the surface of the soil and excrete waste deeper in the soil as they dig. In this way they help break down organic matter and recycle nutrients. An acre (0.41 hectares) of rich soil may contain as many as one million earthworms!

Most of Earth's surface is covered by a layer of soil. It may vary from $\frac{1}{5}$ inch (5mm) thick in mountain regions to 6 feet (2m) deep in farming areas. Different soils have different qualities. Desert soils are sandy and dry. Worms do not like these conditions, so the breakdown of organic material by bacteria is slow in these areas. This dry soil has few nutrients and cannot support many plants.

In contrast, most farms and gardens have richer soil. It comes about either because farmers have added nutrients, such as compost and manure, to the soil, or because they have to grow special crops that help return the nutrients to the soil. Regular digging also helps add oxygen and water to the ground, just as worms do. That speeds up the decomposition (breaking down) of organic material.

Dust Bowl

Soil erosion is the removal of the top layer of the soil by wind or rain. This top layer, called the topsoil, contains a large amount of the organic material that is in the process of breaking down and most of the nutrients plants use to grow.

The topsoil can be damaged or destroyed in various ways. For example, if too many cattle or sheep feed off one area, all the plants will be eaten and the topsoil left exposed. The topsoil can then be blown

or washed away, and the soil that is left will not contain enough nutrients to grow crops.

In the 1930s the livelihood of tens of thousands of farmers in the American Midwest was destroyed when there was a serious and long-term drought. During the drought the plants died, and the topsoil blew away, making it impossible to grow new crops. A large area of the Midwest was turned into a "Dust Bowl" (above).

ACTIVITY 2
AIR POLLUTION

All sorts of substances, from invisible chemicals to smoke particles, are released into the air by human activity and travel all around the world. That has a huge effect on the quality of the air and can cause problems.

Most people do not think of the air as part of their environment or ecosystem, but it is very important. Without the oxygen present in the air much of the life on Earth could not exist. Animals take oxygen into their bodies and use it to break down food and release energy. Plants also use oxygen to release energy from their food.

The air we breathe is actually made up of many different gases, not just oxygen. In fact, the most common gas in air is nitrogen, which makes up 78 percent of air. Twenty-one percent of air is oxygen, and the remaining one percent includes water vapor, carbon dioxide, nitrogen dioxide and the noble, unreactive gases—krypton, argon, xenon, neon, radon, and helium.

Although these other gases make up only about one percent of the total amount of air, any increase in the amount of these gases in the air can have a very dangerous effect. Increasingly, large amounts of

Many major cities have a problem with smog, a combination of smoke and fog, as a result of automobile exhaust fumes and coal- and oil-burning factories.

harmful gases are released into the air by the action of humans. This is often called air pollution.

Burning fossil fuels, such as oil, coal, and natural gas, is one of the major causes of air pollution. These fuels are used to create electricity, to run automobiles, to make chemicals and plastics, and to heat homes, offices, and factories. When fossil fuels are burned, waste products are released into the atmosphere through chimneys and exhaust pipes.

Carbon monoxide, a molecule made of one atom each of carbon and oxygen, is one of these waste products. It is formed when fuels burn in a limited air supply, such as in car engines. Carbon monoxide is a toxic gas that stops the red blood cells in animals from carrying oxygen.

Sulfur dioxide is another toxic gas produced by burning fossil fuels, especially coal. Sulfur dioxide in the air is a major cause of breathing problems such as emphysema and asthma.

The ozone layer

At ground level ozone is harmful to life, but in the upper atmosphere it forms a protective layer called the ozone layer. Ozone is important because it filters out most of the Sun's ultraviolet radiation, which can damage plants and animals.

In the 1980s scientists discovered that a hole was forming in the ozone layer over Antarctica. This meant that the amount of ozone in this area was decreasing, which would allow more ultraviolet radiation through. An increase in ultraviolet radiation of just one percent can damage living organisms. Plankton are tiny forms of ocean life that provide food for many sea creatures. They are very sensitive to ultraviolet radiation. If plankton are damaged, the food chains in the oceans would be badly affected. The ozone layer also helps absorb the heat from the Sun. If there is less ozone, then less heat from the Sun is absorbed. This in turn would mean there would be a change in the weather and climate on Earth. The main gases that are causing the hole in the ozone layer are chlorofluorocarbons (CFCs). These gases are used in some aerosol cans and

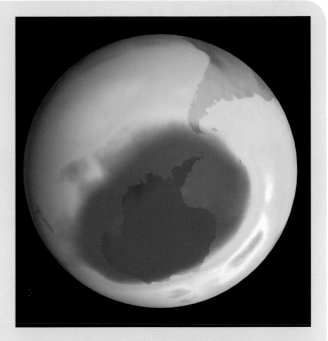

in making polystyrene and in refrigerators. Since scientists discovered that CFCs were causing the problem, some have been removed from the production of these items. However, many scientists believe that there should be an overall ban on products using CFCs.

Particulate matter is another form of air pollution. These tiny particles of unburned fuels (soot) and other materials are produced by engines and factories. They combine with other pollutants and dust in the air and are easily inhaled. They coat the lungs, making breathing difficult and causing many diseases.

Some of the smoke from cars is in the form of hydrocarbons. These unburned fuels react with a gas called nitrogen oxide, and with sunlight, to form ozone. In the upper atmosphere ozone is beneficial, but at ground level smog is caused when fog combines with ozone and other gases. It can irritate the eyes and lungs, cause bronchitis (inflammation of the air passages in the lungs), and destroy crops and wildlife. Scientists believe air pollution causes 3,000 deaths in the United States and thousands more deaths around the world each year.

The gases causing air pollution are invisible, but we can see particulate matter. This experiment will help you see how clean the air around you is.

Lead poisoning

In some countries gasoline contains lead, which is given off in car exhausts. Lead is added to gas to make the engine run better. Some factories also give off lead as a waste product. Lead is a poisonous element that can cause brain damage in children. Many cyclists now wear masks to keep them from breathing car exhaust, which may contain lead.

ACTIVITY

Dirty Air

Goals

1. **See how dirty the air is.**
2. **Compare and measure the amounts of dirt in the air.**

What you will need:

- *thick, stiff white paper*
- *hole punch*
- *string*
- *petroleum jelly*
- *magnifying glass*

Handy hints

Make sure that you attach the paper so that it can turn freely. One way of measuring the total amount of dirt more accurately is by drawing a squared grid on the card in pen before smearing the jelly, and figuring out how much dirt has collected in each square. In this way you can create graphs of the dirt that is collected.

1 Punch a hole at the edge of the paper using the hole punch.

2 Cut a length of string, and thread it through the hole in the paper. Tie a double knot in the string to hold it securely on the paper.

Catalytic converter

The most successful way of reducing pollution from a car exhaust is to attach a device called a catalytic converter. It is put in the exhaust of the car and converts 90 percent of the harmful hydrocarbons, nitrogen oxide, and carbon monoxide into less harmful carbon dioxide, nitrogen, and water. It works effectively if unleaded gas is used.

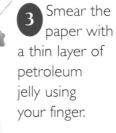

3 Smear the paper with a thin layer of petroleum jelly using your finger.

4 Place the paper outside in the open air, near a road. Attach it firmly by its string to a fence post or similar permanent object using a thumbtack. Leave it overnight.

Troubleshooting

What should I do if nothing collects on the paper?

If you cannot see anything on the paper, you should first check that you have smeared enough petroleum jelly on it, and then leave it out for another night, perhaps closer to a busier road.

5 The next morning inspect the paper using first just your naked eye, and then the magnifying glass. How much dirt has collected on the piece of paper?

FOLLOW-UP ⟨ Dirty air ⟩

Try putting papers in different areas near where you live: by a busy main road, in the park, in your garden—and then measure and compare the dirt that is collected. Which areas are the cleanest? Which are the dirtiest? You can draw up a map of the area to show where the cleaner air is.

Find out who in your neighborhood has the dirtiest car exhaust by carrying out another simple experiment. You will need an adult to help you with this because the cars need to be started. Cut the toe off of a clean white sock, and place it over the car's exhaust pipe. (Only place it on a car that has not been running—exhaust pipes get hot.) Now get an adult to start the car. Let the car run for one minute, and then stop the engine. Wait for the exhaust pipe to cool completely before removing the sock. Turn the sock inside out, and you will see the dirt given out by the car's exhaust. Try this on several friends' cars in your area, and build up a chart of who has the cleanest and dirtiest cars.

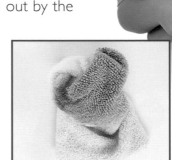

● *Make sure you cut the toe end off the sock before you put it over the exhaust.*

ANALYSIS ⟨ Air pollution ⟩

You should have found a lot of dirt and dust on the paper. Some of it is from the ground, but a lot of it will be particles thrown out from car exhausts. Under a magnifying glass the particles from a car exhaust will appear darker in color than the dirt and dust from the ground. These car exhaust particles are burned material from car engines. If large amounts of these materials are breathed in over many years, they can cause serious health problems.

If you compared papers placed near busy streets to papers placed in a park or countryside, you probably found that both papers were dirty, but the one near the street had more particles from car exhaust. If it was dry, you may have found lots of dust on the paper, too. Breathing large amounts over a long period of time can also be dangerous; dust coats the lungs and makes breathing harder. That is why dust is sometimes considered air pollution.

Pollution from car exhausts can be best reduced by using less fuel. At home and at work people use large amounts of energy, mostly produced by burning fossil fuels like gasoline. If more people used public transportation and left their cars at home, if trucks returned full rather than empty after delivering their loads, and if buildings were better insulated, then the amounts of fossil fuel burned, and the levels of car emissions, would be reduced. Emissions can also be reduced by regular engine maintenance and by driving more smoothly and slowly.

ACTIVITY 3
THE GREENHOUSE EFFECT

Earth's atmosphere may be getting warmer. The most likely cause of this global warming is air pollution—mainly higher levels of carbon dioxide— and the greenhouse effect, a natural feature of the atmosphere.

Earth is surrounded by an airy blanket called the atmosphere—a mixture of gases, water vapor, and dust. The atmosphere traps air, moisture, and heat near the planet's surface. It supports life, protects Earth from small meteorites (which bounce off the atmosphere), and acts as a shield against harmful radiation from the Sun. The atmosphere is vital. Without it Earth would be like the Moon— airless, waterless, and lifeless.

The proportion of gases in the atmosphere is very important. Some of these gases are called greenhouse gases, one of the most important being carbon dioxide. Carbon dioxide helps trap heat from the Sun and keep it from escaping into space—just as glass traps warmth in a greenhouse.

For millions of years the amount of carbon dioxide in the atmosphere stayed in balance. However, burning fossil fuels, such as oil and coal, releases carbon dioxide and greatly increases the amount of carbon dioxide in the atmosphere. In the past

◗ **Dense rain forest canopies help balance the amount of carbon dioxide in the air because the trees use carbon dioxide during the process of photosynthesis.**

vast forests helped keep the balance by using the carbon dioxide during photosynthesis and changing it to oxygen. Cutting and burning many of the huge forests means those trees can no longer exchange carbon dioxide for oxygen. As the proportion of greenhouse gases in the atmosphere increases, more and more heat is trapped near Earth's surface, an effect called global warming.

The world's climates change all the time. More than 65 million years ago, when dinosaurs roamed the planet, there were no polar ice caps, and tropical vegetation grew in temperate regions like Europe and North America. About one million years ago ice covered much of Earth. However, climate change occurred slowly in the past—now it has been sped up by human action.

Trapping Heat

Goals

1. **Explore the idea of a greenhouse and how a layer of material increases the temperature.**

2. **Understand better how Earth's atmosphere works.**

What you will need:

- shoebox
- black paint and paintbrush
- 4 thermometers
- tape
- 12 cork or rubber stoppers
- plastic or glass panes cut to fit in the shoebox
- notebook and pen

1 Paint the inside of the shoebox black, and let it dry.

2 Tape one of the thermometers onto the floor of the shoebox at one end.

3 Place four corks in the box—one at each corner, and place one pane of glass on the corks.

Handy hints

Make sure each thermometer is exposed to the same amount of sunlight. For a more visual experiment, place an ice cube next to each thermometer, and see which one melts the fastest. Draw a graph or chart showing the differences in temperature.

4 Tape the second thermometer to the pane of glass—in a different spot from where you taped the first thermometer. Place four more corks on this pane—one at each corner, and place a second pane of glass on the corks.

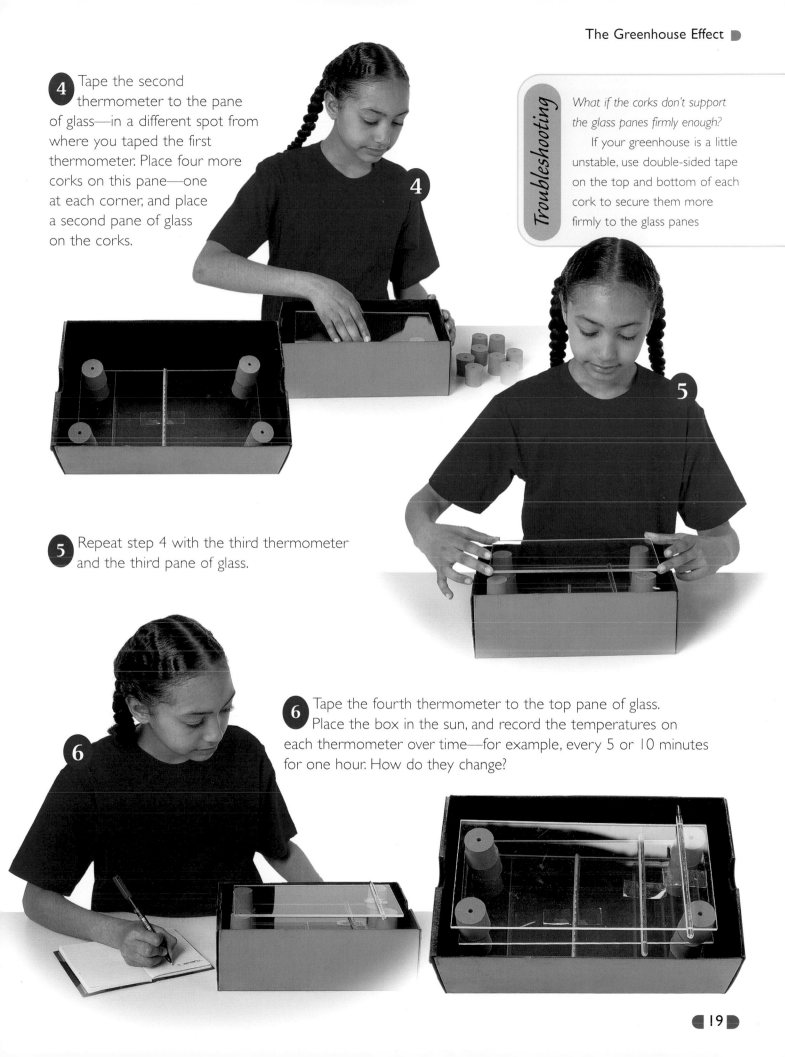

Troubleshooting

What if the corks don't support the glass panes firmly enough?

If your greenhouse is a little unstable, use double-sided tape on the top and bottom of each cork to secure them more firmly to the glass panes

5 Repeat step 4 with the third thermometer and the third pane of glass.

6 Tape the fourth thermometer to the top pane of glass. Place the box in the sun, and record the temperatures on each thermometer over time—for example, every 5 or 10 minutes for one hour. How do they change?

FOLLOW-UP Trapping heat

You can also demon-strate how carbon dioxide levels affect Earth by carrying out another experiment.

Take two identical plastic bottles. Half-fill one with tap water and the other with carbonated (fizzy) water. (If you don't have carbonated water, you can make it by dropping an Alka-Seltzer™ tablet into tap water.) Take the temperature of both bottles, and then put them out in the sun. Leave them in the sun for 15 minutes, and then take the temperatures again. Which bottle is hotter? Is it what you expected?

ANALYSIS
The greenhouse effect

The temperatures under the panes of glass should be higher than in the open air because the glass slows the escape of heat from the box. In Earth's atmosphere this effect is caused by greenhouse gases. Without these gases Earth would be too cold to support life; but if the layer of greenhouse gases increases, then heat cannot escape—and Earth becomes too hot to support life.

There are about 30 greenhouse gases, but 40 percent of global warming is caused by just one gas—carbon dioxide. Large amounts of this gas are released when fossil fuels, such as oil, gas, and coal, are burned. The amounts of carbon dioxide in the atmosphere are very small, but they are rising fast. Since 1850 the amount of carbon dioxide in the atmosphere has risen by more than 50 percent.

As the amount of carbon dioxide increases, more heat is trapped, and temperatures rise over the whole planet. Scientists believe that the average temperature on Earth will rise by 2.7 °F (1.5 °C) in the next 50 years.

Plants take in carbon dioxide and give off oxygen. The most important areas for helping reduce carbon dioxide in the atmosphere are

Natural heat trap

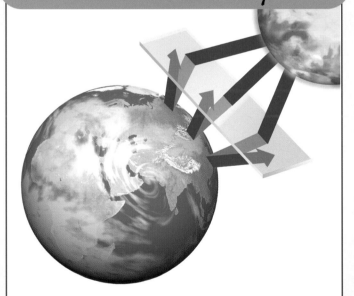

Earth's atmosphere acts like the glass of a greenhouse. The Sun's rays pass through the atmosphere, and some are reflected back into space by clouds. Others are absorbed by the Earth's surface, and infrared heat is given out. Some of this heat is trapped in the atmosphere, warming the planet, and the rest escapes. Less heat escapes if there are more greenhouse gases in the atmosphere.

Global warming

The greenhouse effect is the natural process that keeps Earth warm and allows life to flourish. Global warming, however, describes the heating up of Earth. Rapid temperature changes have a huge effect on all life on Earth. Even a temperature rise of just 1.8 °F (1°C) would cause sea levels to rise due to the expansion of water as it warms and ice melting at the North and South Poles. With scientists predicting rises in sea levels of 6½ feet (2m), many seaside areas, including towns, would simply disappear under water. Other effects of global warming would include warmer and wetter winters and summers, which cause more floods and storms and the spread of tropical diseases. Some plants would no longer grow in places they were once well adapted for. That would affect the animals, including people, that depend on the plants for shelter and food.

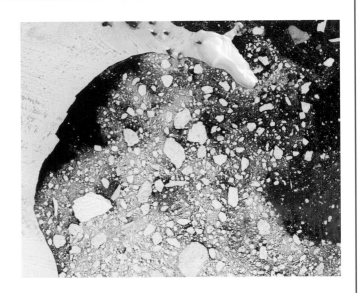

🔲 *If Earth's temperature rises by even a tiny amount, the polar ice (above) will begin to melt.*

those where there are large numbers of trees, such as rain forests. They also play an important role in many ecosystems, holding water and releasing it slowly over hundreds of miles. Half of the world's rain forests have already been destroyed, and they are still being cut down. One reason is the world's increasing population—people need to find new places to live. Rain forests are also destroyed to make new farmlands for grazing cattle; and some of the rain forest wood is used to make things.

In certain areas people are trying to stop this destruction of the rain forests. Many places have tree-planting projects in which timber merchants have to replace the trees with more than the number that they cut down. The problem is that these hardwood trees take decades to grow, while the effects of their destruction are noticed in just a few years.

Rain forest land is cleared for new housing or for grazing animals by burning (left). The minerals stored in the plants turn to ash, and the root systems are destroyed. This allows rain to wash away the topsoil. Often, areas cleared in this way, which were once rich in life, can no longer support life. Many people are campaigning to stop further destruction of the rain forests. However, until countries agree internationally that the destruction must stop, these vital parts of Earth's ecosystem will continue to be destroyed.

🔲 *Rain forests support the richest variety of living organisms on Earth and are a valuable source of plants and fungi used in medicine—but only if left undisturbed.*

ACTIVITY 4
WATER, WATER EVERYWHERE

Water circulates through every ecosystem, linking them together as it circulates between the oceans, the atmosphere, and the land. All life depends on water and is put in peril when water is polluted.

The oceans, covering 70 percent of Earth's surface, form large biomes. Within these large biomes there are many ecosystems, such as coral reefs and kelp forests, each with an environment of its own. The organisms that live in the seas are as varied as the organisms on land.

Some of the habitats within oceans are similar to habitats on Earth's surface. For example, there are sandy deserts where there are comparatively few living creatures. There are also huge mountain ranges and deep trenches.

Many other ocean habitats are completely different from habitats on land. Oceans contain unique and spectacular underwater landscapes built from varieties of coral reefs. Coral reefs occur in areas of warm, tropical water and are made by living creatures. These tiny animals build hard skeletons. Over hundreds of years new corals grow on top of the skeletons of dead corals, and a reef is built layer by

■ Nearly three-quarters of Earth's surface is covered with water. Water is vital for all life.

layer. Small fish feed on the live corals, and the small fish are then eaten by larger fish. Many fish make a home in the dead coral or use it as a good place to hide. Coral reefs provide food and shelter to thousands of fish species.

Ocean food webs all depend on microscopic plantlike algae called phytoplankton. Most live very close to the ocean surface because they need the energy in sunlight to grow, and there is more sunlight near the surface of the water. Phytoplankton release oxygen as a by-product. They are responsible for producing 70 percent of the world's oxygen supply.

The phytoplankton are eaten by microscopic animals called zooplankton, which in turn are food for small fish. The small fish are then eaten by larger animals, and so on throughout the food web.

Pollution of the oceans is a major problem. More than 80 percent of ocean pollution comes from human land-based activities. In the past most of the waste that humans dumped into the sea consisted of small amounts of natural substances such as sewage and food waste. They decayed over time and were easily absorbed into the ocean food chain.

Today, a lot more of these substances are dumped into the oceans, along with metals and plastics that take hundreds of years to decay. In addition, industrial waste containing poisonous chemicals is now also dumped into oceans and rivers. These chemicals kill all types of sea life, large and small. The chemicals we use on farms also destroy sea life. Farmers spray their fields with large amounts of pesticides and fertilizers, rain then washes these chemicals into the rivers, and they are eventually carried to the sea.

A lot of ocean pollution is caused by offshore oil drilling and oil transportation. Oil spilled from tankers or oil rigs is one of the most harmful pollutants and also one of the most difficult to clean up. The oil kills ocean plants, fish, and animals, and destroys ocean habitat. The activity on the following pages illustrates the problems created by ocean oil spills.

Algal blooms

Algae are water-dwelling organisms that include phytoplankton and seaweeds. Some pollutants make algae grow very quickly, forming masses of organisms called "algal blooms," like this one. When the algae die, bacteria feed on them, taking oxygen from the water and killing fish.

Water cycle

Earth's water continuously circulates between the oceans, the atmosphere, and the land. Water evaporates from the surface of the sea as invisible water vapor (1). Along with other gases in the air it cools when it rises. The water vapor becomes visible as cloud (2) when it cools enough to turn into droplets of water or crystals of ice. Rainfall from clouds seeps into the ground and gathers in streams and rivers (3). It returns to the oceans, carrying minerals dissolved from the soil. It also carries polluting chemicals that have been discharged from factories and cities.

Oil Slick

Goals

1. **Explore some of the effects of oil pollution.**
2. **Demonstrate the difficulties of removing oil from rocks, sand, animals, and birds.**

What you will need:

- *clear container*
- *water*
- *engine oil, provided by an adult*
- *rubber gloves*
- *feathers*
- *bowl*
- *warm water*
- *dishwashing detergent*

1 Half-fill the clear container with water.

Safety tip

Oil and other cleaning materials are poisonous, so do not taste or drink anything. Use safety gloves at all times, and wash your hands thoroughly after the activity. When cleaning up after the experiment, make sure that anything that still has oil on it is set out for one of your neighborhood's oil recycling days. Do not pour the oil down the drain, since that contributes to the oil pollution problem.

2 Carefully pour a little oil onto the surface of the water.

3 The oil will settle on the surface of the water. Wearing the rubber gloves, take the feather, and dip it into the oil and water.

Handy hint
This is a messy activity, and you need to carry it out on surfaces that are protected against both water and oil stains. Cover all surfaces with a thick layer of newspaper before starting the activity.

4 Remove the feather, and place it in the bowl of warm water. Try to clean off the oil using just the water. Does the feather get clean?

5 Now pour some detergent or dishwashing liquid into the bowl of warm water.

6 Try to clean the feather using the dishwashing liquid. Is it any easier? Repeat the experiment using fake fur.

FOLLOW-UP Oil slick

Oil spilled in the sea will eventually be washed up onto a beach or rocks. To see the effect of this, take a small container, and place some sand and small rocks in it. Pour oil over the sand and rocks, leave them for a few minutes, and then try cleaning the oil off using paper towels, liquid detergent or soap, and warm water. Imagine how much effort it takes to clean up beaches and coastal rocks after they have been polluted by an oil spill.

Try to find different ways of cleaning the sand and rocks. You could try shaking the sand up in a bottle with water and detergent—how well does this work? How do you think a similar thing could be done on a large scale? And what could be done to quickly clean thousands of birds and sea creatures covered in sticky oil?

ANALYSIS
Water, water everywhere

Oil floats on water and spreads rapidly across its surface, creating a thin layer that is called an oil slick. As the oil spreads, the layer becomes thinner and thinner. It is visible as a rainbow-colored sheen on the water. You should have noticed this in your experiment.

Birds and fur-covered animals are at great risk from oil spills. If feathers become covered in oil, they can no longer keep the bird dry. Animals caught in an oil slick will try and clean themselves, often by licking their fur or feathers. If they swallow the oil as they do that, then it will poison them. Large oil slicks kill thousands of birds and animals each year.

After a large oil spill, floating barriers called booms are placed around the spill to keep it from spreading. Boats called skimmers scoop up the oil. Large sponges are also used to soak up the oil. Sometimes the oil is burned off the surface while it is floating on the water.

Chemicals called dispersants are also used to break down the oil. They are very similar to dishwashing detergent. The detergent coats the oil and breaks it up into patches of detergent-coated drops, allowing light and oxygen to reach sea creatures below the surface. These drops are then scooped or soaked up.

On the beach, after the detergent is applied, high-pressure water hoses wash the oil off the rocks, and vacuum trucks suck it up.

■ *On a beach hit by an oil spill a pool of oil is sucked up into a tanker truck. Afterward the really difficult job will begin—removing oil from miles of rocks and sand.*

ACTIVITY 5
ACID RAIN

Acid rain is polluted snow, fog, mist, or rain. It is a serious environmental threat because it can cause ill health, damage crops and trees, kill fish and plants in lakes and rivers, and even dissolve stone buildings.

Acid rain causes worldwide problems because one country's pollution can damage another's environment.

Most of the rain that falls to the ground is good for us and for other living things, but the rain can also be polluted. One of the causes of this pollution is the smoke from factories, power plants, and car exhausts. Smoke from burning fossil fuels, such as oil, coal, and natural gas, contains many harmful substances. Two of them, sulfur dioxide and nitrogen oxide, can cause a lot of damage. When they enter the atmosphere, they are absorbed by the water vapor in the atmosphere. The water vapor then becomes weak sulfuric acid or nitric acid. This acid falls to the ground as rain, snow, or mist and is called acid rain.

Acids are corrosive. When they come into contact with certain materials, they chemically react, and the original material is eaten away. Acid rain causes damage to forests, pollutes lakes, and corrodes buildings. When acid rain falls on the leaves of trees in a forest, the leaves are damaged and can no longer make food for the tree. When the rain falls on the soil, the soil becomes acidic, and it is very difficult for plants to grow in. Acid rain is taken up by plants, and eventually they die.

Acid rain can also enter lakes and streams. If water becomes too acidic, then animals like fish and frogs can no longer live in those areas.

People can also be affected by acid rain. Fish from acid lakes can contain poisonous metals that have been dissolved out of the soil by acid rain. If people eat these fish, then they will be poisoned.

Not all rain is acid, so it is difficult to watch acid rain do damage. But you can duplicate the damaging effect of acid rain using some common acids.

Acids at Work

Goals

1. **Show how acids react with soft rocks to cause erosion damage.**
2. **Demonstrate the effect of acid on plants.**

What you will need:

- *5 clear jars*
- *lemon juice*
- *vinegar*
- *water*
- *3 pieces of chalk*
- *2 cut flowers*
- *houseplant with wide leaves*
- *soft cloth*

■ Experiment I

1 Half-fill one jar with lemon juice.

2 Half-fill a second jar with vinegar and a third with water. Drop a piece of chalk into each jar.

3 In which jar does the chalk dissolve fastest? In which jar does the chalk dissolve slowest?

Handy hints

You can decorate pieces of chalk by covering them with wax and scratching a pattern into the surface. The acid vinegar will attack only the exposed piece of chalk but will not penetrate the wax. This process is used to etch metals such as copper.

Experiment 2

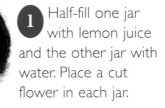

1 Half-fill one jar with lemon juice and the other jar with water. Place a cut flower in each jar.

2 Watch what happens to the flowers over the next 24 hours, and record the results.

Experiment 3

1 Take the house plant, and wipe the leaves on one side of the plant with vinegar. Wipe the leaves on the other side of the plant with water.

2 Watch what happens to the leaves over the next 24 hours, and record the results.

FOLLOW-UP

Acids at work

Vinegar and lemon juice are mild acids. They both react with the chalk to dissolve it and produce new chemicals as they react. The pH scale measures how acidic a substance is. The scale goes from 0 to 14. Neutral substances such as pure water have a pH of 7. The strongest acids have a pH of 0. Alkalis (or bases) have a pH starting above 7, with the strongest alkalis at pH14. Alkalis neutralize acids and can prevent some of their harmful effects.

To find out how acidic or alkaline a substance is, you can make your own pH indicator from red cabbage.

What you will need:
hot water
cutting board
saucepan
strainer
red cabbage
jar
knife
cool water

1 Be very careful using the knife and hot water. Fill the pan with tap water. Chop the red cabbage leaves, and place them in the water. Simmer the cabbage on the stove for 10 minutes. Leave it to cool.

2 Strain the liquid into a jar, and dilute it with extra water until you have a deep purple liquid. This liquid will be the test for acids and alkalis.

3 Pour some vinegar into a glass, and add some of the cabbage water. Acids should turn the cabbage water pink.

4 Pour some baking soda into another glass, and add some of the cabbage water. It should turn blue, showing that baking soda is an alkali.

You can use this indicator to test other materials and find out their pH. Make your own scale using the different colors that it produces. Test the water in your tap and in any local lakes, rivers, or streams. You can also collect rain water in a glass during a storm and test it for its acidity. Is the rainwater very acidic?

ANALYSIS
Acid rain

Lakes that are very polluted with acid rain can have a pH as low as 4, which is too acidic to support life. In some countries acid rain in the water supply has become a major problem. In the 1980s the number of fish in Norwegian lakes began decreasing rapidly. Scientists found that all the lakes had very high acid levels, and some had a pH as low as 4.5. However, the pollution that was causing the problem for Norway was coming from other countries. The pollution that creates acid rain can be carried

Acid rain attacks certain materials faster than others. Many statues are carved from soft rocks, and they are very quickly damaged by acid rain.

on the air for days before it finally returns to the ground. The damage that the rain causes may be a long way from where it started. Norway's problems were solved by adding alkaline chemicals to the water to balance, or neutralize, the acidic effects and allow life to return to the poisoned lakes.

Acid rain can be reduced by putting filters in power plant chimneys and catalytic converters in vehicle exhaust pipes. Countries can also try to reduce the dangerous pollutants that cause acid rain.

Acid rain cycle

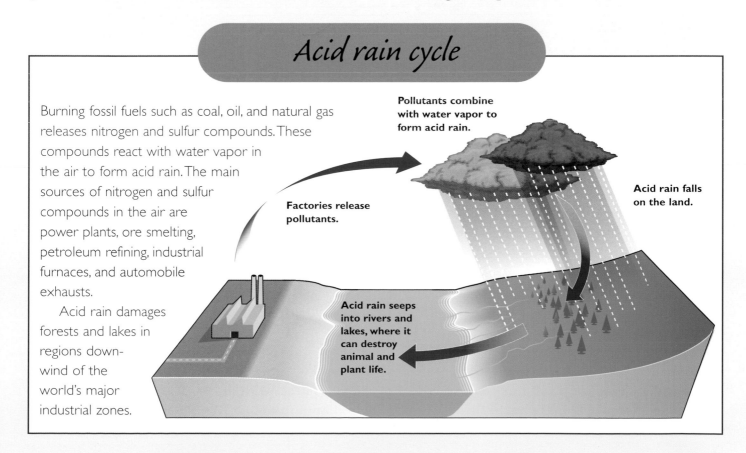

Burning fossil fuels such as coal, oil, and natural gas releases nitrogen and sulfur compounds. These compounds react with water vapor in the air to form acid rain. The main sources of nitrogen and sulfur compounds in the air are power plants, ore smelting, petroleum refining, industrial furnaces, and automobile exhausts.

Acid rain damages forests and lakes in regions downwind of the world's major industrial zones.

Pollutants combine with water vapor to form acid rain.

Factories release pollutants.

Acid rain falls on the land.

Acid rain seeps into rivers and lakes, where it can destroy animal and plant life.

ACTIVITY 6
RENEWABLE ENERGY

If you strike a match and let it burn on a saucer until it turns black, the flame goes out. The match has given out all its energy. Outside, the Sun shines, and the wind blows every day. Their energy can be used over and over.

The source of energy for all living things on Earth is the Sun. Plants use the Sun's energy to convert carbon dioxide and water into food to help them grow. Other organisms, such as animals and fungi, feed on plants. Heat energy from the Sun helps create different climates around the world, and that in turn affects which organisms live where.

People use energy from food, but we also use other sources of energy to make heat and electricity and to power industry. Most of this energy comes from the burning of fossil fuels.

Fossil fuels come from the slow decomposition of plants and animals that lived hundreds of millions of years ago. Over millions of years the heat inside the Earth and the pressure of other material build-

■ *Wind turbines grouped on a hill where there are strong and steady winds can generate a lot of electricity. This is the world's largest wind farm, with 6,000 windmills, located at Altamont Pass, California.*

ing up on top of the dead organisms turned the carbon in these organisms into coal, gas, and oil. That is why we call them fossil fuels.

Because fossil fuels take millions of years to form but are used up very quickly, we will eventually run out of them. Fossil fuels also give out dangerous waste products when they are burned. Some of these wastes contribute to the warming of Earth (see Activity 3, pages 17 to 21), and many of them are deadly to plants and animals, including humans.

Another source of energy is nuclear reactions. Nuclear power plants are very efficient, but the waste they produce is deadly and is difficult to get rid of. Also, accidents at nuclear power plants can kill large numbers of people very quickly.

For these reasons scientists are constantly looking for alternative sources of energy that will not run out or pollute the environment. One renewable power source is the Sun's energy, also called solar energy, which can be used to produce both heat and electricity (see box, right).

The Sun's rays have to be concentrated on one area before their energy can be used to create power. In large solar power plants a large number of mirrors, called an array, collect the Sun's rays. Heat collected by the array is then used to heat water. The water changes into steam, which then turns large fans called turbines. The turbines then operate a generator that creates electricity. The Sun moves through the sky as the day goes on, and so the mirrors turn to follow the Sun in order to keep the rays focused and to keep producing electricity.

Buildings can also be equipped with solar panels. The solar panels are placed on the roof to catch as much sun as possible. They have glass or plastic

■ *A house equipped with solar panels saves money on fuel bills and helps keep the environment clean.*

Solar cells

Solar panels, like those attached to the roof of the house below, left, are made of many solar cells. Solar cells (photovoltaic cells) are made from a thin layer of silicon placed next to a thinner layer of silicon mixed with a small amount of an element called boron. When light hits the top layer of silicon, electrons from the second layer travel across to the top layer. This flow of electrons creates electricity.

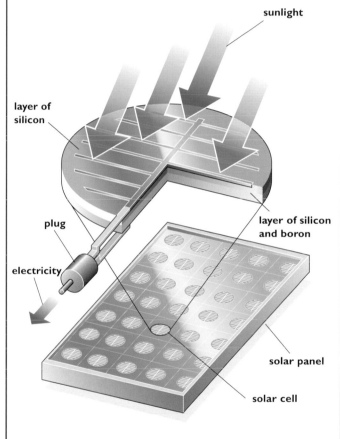

sunlight

layer of silicon

plug

electricity

layer of silicon and boron

solar panel

solar cell

panels that are painted black. (Black absorbs more heat than white.) Water pipes run behind the glass. The pipes sit on layers of foil that help reflect and concentrate the Sun's heat. Cold water flowing through the pipes is heated by the Sun's rays and then flows down to a hot-water tank where it can run into the heating system or to hot-water taps.

The following activity will let you see for yourself how effective the Sun is at heating. You can use the information you learn to create more efficient methods of solar heating.

Energy from the Sun

Goals

1. **Discover the most effective way of soaking up the Sun's heat energy.**

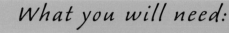

What you will need:

- *two plastic bottles*
- *two balloons*
- *two rubber bands*
- *black poster paint*
- *white poster paint*
- *newspaper*
- *lamp or sunny day*
- *paint brushes*

1 Paint one of the plastic bottles white, and paint the other bottle black (see Handy hints).

2 Place a balloon over the neck of each bottle. Use a rubber band to hold the balloons in place.

Handy hints

When painting the bottles, always make sure you cover your work surface with newspaper first. Secure the balloons tightly to the neck of the bottle because you do not want the balloon to come off or air to leak out.

Troubleshooting

What if nothing happens to the balloons?
You may not notice any changes in your balloons if it is a cool day, or if you do not have the bottles in direct (overhead) sunlight. Make sure you are placing the bottles in a sunny place. If there are any leaks or holes in the balloons, you will not see any changes, so make sure the balloons are tightly secured to the bottles.

3 Place both bottles in the sun. Watch what happens to the balloons over the next few minutes.

4 After a few minutes you should see one of the balloons stand upright as the air inside it expands. When this happens, move both bottles into the shade. Now what happens to the balloons?

5 If there is not much sun, don't worry, you can still perform the activity. Use a desk lamp instead of the Sun. Position the lamp so that it is shining directly on the balloons and is about 6 inches (15cm) above them

FOLLOW-UP

Energy from the Sun

Solar arrays are groups of parabolic (curved) mirrors that focus the Sun's rays and make them stronger.

You can see the effect of this for yourself by making your own, simple parabolic mirror.

Take a piece of thin cardboard, and cover it with aluminum foil. Bend the cardboard so that it makes a curve (below, left). Place it behind the bottles so that the sun shines onto it. Do the balloons inflate more quickly with the Sun's rays focused behind the bottles?

You can test the effectiveness of other colors on absorbing the Sun's rays by painting more

bottles different colors. Try the experiment again with a purple bottle (below) or a blue bottle. What colors work best?

ANALYSIS

Renewable energy

You should have found that in a given amount of time the balloon on the black bottle expanded more than the balloon on the white bottle. Black absorbs more heat than white. As the air inside the bottles heats up, it expands and inflates the balloon.

If you performed the follow-up activity with the parabolic mirror, you should have noticed that the balloons filled much quicker than without the mirror. The mirror focused the Sun's rays and increased the amount of heat energy that was directed onto the bottles.

Other types of heat energy can also be used to create power. For example, the heat deep in the Earth can be converted into electricity.

More than 1,200 miles (2,000km) below the surface lies the outer core of Earth. Made of liquid metals, temperatures here are thought to be at least 7,232 °F (4,000 °C). Where Earth's crust is very thin, molten rock and superheated steam erupt to the surface through volcanoes and fissures in the rock. The heat that comes to the surface can be used for heating and to generate electricity. It is geothermal power.

To produce geothermal power, cold water is pumped through boreholes 6,500 feet (1,980m) deep. The water fills small cracks in the deep, hot rocks. Once the water is heated by the rocks, it is pumped back to the surface at temperatures of 390 °F (200 °C). Because the water is under pressure, it does not boil. As it returns to the surface and reaches normal atmospheric pressure, the water turns rapidly into steam. This steam turns turbines in generators that produce electricity.

The power of the wind can also be used to generate electricity. The wind is used to turn large moving blades (turbines), similar to fan blades, and these blades then turn a generator, to produce electricity. The blades can be up to 330 feet (100m) across to capture as much of the wind as possible. They are equipped with sensors that turn them into the oncoming wind. One large wind turbine can produce enough electricity to supply a small town. For larger areas a number of turbines are grouped together in what are called wind farms.

🔋 *This geothermal pool in Iceland makes a warm swimming pool. The naturally hot water is also used to run the geothermal power plant in the background.*

Water power

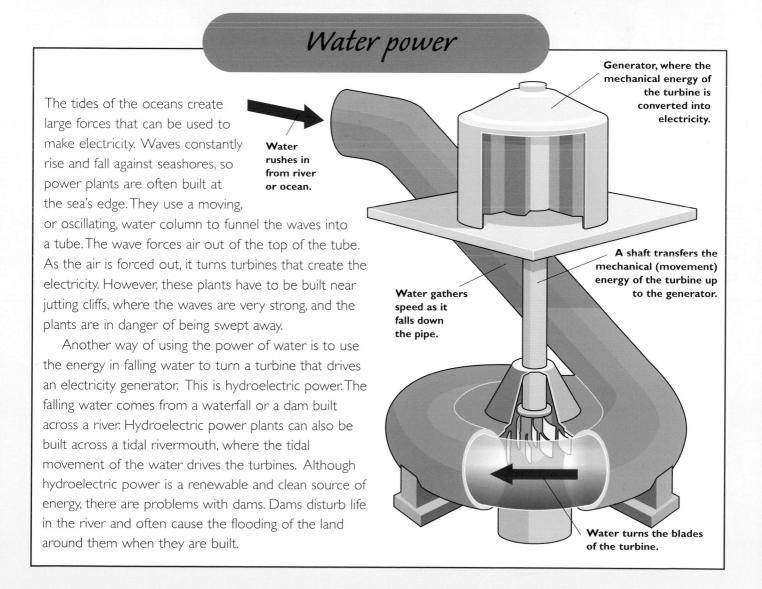

The tides of the oceans create large forces that can be used to make electricity. Waves constantly rise and fall against seashores, so power plants are often built at the sea's edge. They use a moving, or oscillating, water column to funnel the waves into a tube. The wave forces air out of the top of the tube. As the air is forced out, it turns turbines that create the electricity. However, these plants have to be built near jutting cliffs, where the waves are very strong, and the plants are in danger of being swept away.

Another way of using the power of water is to use the energy in falling water to turn a turbine that drives an electricity generator. This is hydroelectric power. The falling water comes from a waterfall or a dam built across a river. Hydroelectric power plants can also be built across a tidal rivermouth, where the tidal movement of the water drives the turbines. Although hydroelectric power is a renewable and clean source of energy, there are problems with dams. Dams disturb life in the river and often cause the flooding of the land around them when they are built.

Water rushes in from river or ocean.

Generator, where the mechanical energy of the turbine is converted into electricity.

A shaft transfers the mechanical (movement) energy of the turbine up to the generator.

Water gathers speed as it falls down the pipe.

Water turns the blades of the turbine.

ACTIVITY 7
THE SECRET LIFE OF PLANTS

Plants make their own food using the energy in sunlight in a process called photosynthesis. Plants are the starting point for most food chains on Earth. Without plants most other living things would not be able to exist.

Plants form a very important part of almost every ecosystem. While animals get their energy by eating other animals or plants, plants get their energy directly from the Sun. Using the energy in sunlight, plants build energy-rich compounds called carbohydrates from water, minerals, and carbon dioxide gas. This process is called photosynthesis. Compounds called carbohydrates, which include sugars and starch, are the food reserves of the plant. They are also food for many animals, including humans. The food chains in most ecosystems begin with plants. Even in oceans food chains begin with tiny plantlike algae and plankton.

Without plants and algae, and photosynthesis, there would be no oxygen gas in Earth's atmosphere. Most organisms on Earth need oxygen to survive. Oxygen gas is given off by plants and algae as a by-product of photosynthesis.

PHOTOSYNTHESIS

Photosynthesis takes place in the leaves of plants. Plant leaves contain a green substance called chlorophyll, which traps the sunlight needed to make carbohydrates. The cells in plant leaves are arranged so the maximum surface area is exposed to the Sun. The leaves are also thin, so gases and other substances can pass through them easily. The top layer of a leaf is called the epidermis. It is a single layer of cells that covers the leaf like a skin. The epidermal cells are usually transparent, to

◀ *Redwoods (left) grow very tall so their branches and leaves are lifted high above the dark forest floor and fully exposed to the sunlight.*

Making sugars

Plants use the energy from sunlight to make sugars in a process called photosynthesis. Inside the tightly packed palisade cells in the leaves of a plant are structures called chloroplasts in which photosynthesis takes place. Chloroplasts contain a green pigment called chlorophyll. Chlorophyll traps the Sun's energy, which the plant uses to make molecules of glucose from water and carbon dioxide. Oxygen is released as a by-product. The glucose provides energy for the plant.

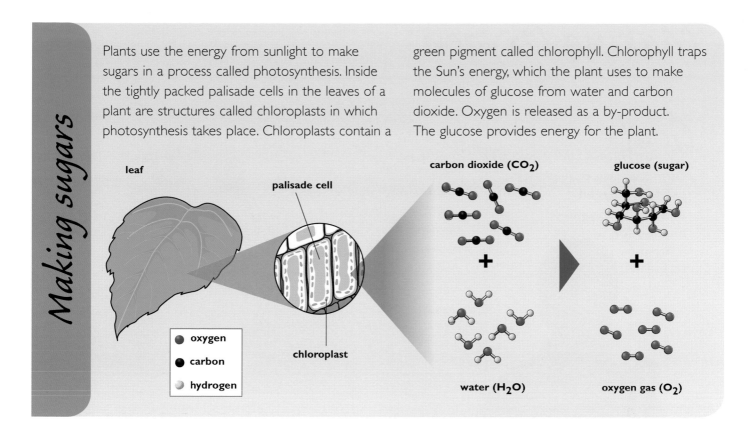

leaf

palisade cell

chloroplast

- ● oxygen
- ● carbon
- ○ hydrogen

carbon dioxide (CO_2)

water (H_2O)

glucose (sugar)

oxygen gas (O_2)

allow the sunlight through. The epidermis protects the cells inside and helps waterproof the leaf. Below the epidermis is a layer of cells called the palisade cells, which are closely packed to receive as much light as possible. These cells contain microscopic structures called chloroplasts, which contain the pigment chlorophyll. Chlorophyll is a molecule that absorbs the energy from light. It also reflects light in the green wavelength, which is what gives many plants their green color.

Plants, like animals, need oxygen to release energy from their food. At night plants take in oxygen and give off carbon dioxide. As the Sun rises, the process of photosynthesis begins. During the day the plants take in carbon dioxide, water, and sunlight. The plant uses the energy from sunlight to split water into hydrogen and oxygen, and carbon dioxide into carbon and oxygen. The carbon, hydrogen, and some of the oxygen then join to make a type of sugar called glucose, and the leftover oxygen is released (see box above). The glucose is carried around the plant. Some glucose is used for energy and to help the plant grow. The glucose that is not used is joined together to make starch and stored for later use.

Sunflowers

Like many other plants, sunflowers (below) turn during the day to follow the Sun's progress across the sky. That allows the sunflower to take full advantage of the sunlight. Sunflowers often grow close together, but they also grow tall, to lift their leaves high and away from the other sunflowers.

Making Oxygen

Goals

1. **Demonstrate that plants produce oxygen.**
2. **Show that oxygen is needed for a flame to burn.**

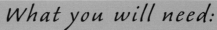

What you will need:

- *one houseplant*
- *two airtight containers large enough to take the houseplant*
- *two tea lights or candles*
- *matches*
- *stopwatch*

1 Place the houseplant on the base of one of the airtight containers.

2 Place one tea light on each base, and have an adult light the tea lights. Make sure the tea light is not beneath any parts of the plant, or they could catch fire.

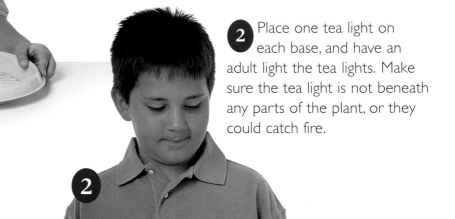

Safety tip

Make sure the containers and lids you use are not made of a material that will burn or melt. Always check with an adult before doing this activity.

Food stores

Different plants store their starch food reserves in different ways. Some plants, such as cabbages, store it in their leaves. Other plants, such as celery, store it in their stems. Carrots and potatoes store starch in their roots. Onions and other bulbs store food in layers, while cereal crops like corn and wheat store their food in seeds. Think about the parts of different plants that you eat. Those parts are where the plant stores its food.

3 Carefully put the lids on the containers, and start your stopwatch.

4 Time how long it takes for each flame to go out. Which flame goes out first?

Troubleshooting

What if the flames do not go out?

Make sure that the containers are sealed properly. If oxygen can get into the containers, the flames will not go out. A very large jar with a screw top would be a good type of container to use.

FOLLOW-UP Making oxygen

Try repeating the activity with other green plants. You can also repeat the activity in the dark to compare how much oxygen the plant gives off at night. Plants that live in water also produce oxygen. That is one way for oxygen to get into water. The leaves on water plants are often feathery to help them catch the carbon dioxide dissolved in water.

You can see the oxygen produced by water plants by carrying out a simple experiment. Place a piece of pondweed in a funnel. Fill a small jar or test tube with water, and place it over the spout of the funnel. Fill a bowl with water, turn the funnel over, and submerge the whole thing in the bowl so that the funnel fills with water. Use a pen to mark the water level on the jar. Put the bowl in the sun. Time how quickly the water in the jar is replaced with oxygen made by the plant.

■ **You can see how water plants produce oxygen during photosynthesis by carrying out this simple experiment.**

Finding the light

Plants are sensitive to their surroundings. This experiment shows how a plant grows toward the light. Use fast-growing plants such as runner beans, sunflowers, vines, or tomatoes. Cut one end off a shoebox, and make slots in the sides as shown. Put your plant in the bottom of the box. Carefully insert pieces of cardboard, or stiff paper, into the slots so that the plant cannot grow straight upward. As it grows, the plant will twist and turn its stem to find the light. This type of plant behavior is called positive phototropism.

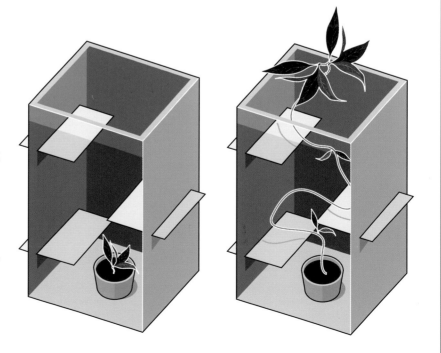

ANALYSIS
The secret life of plants

The candle in the container with the plant should have burned for a longer time than the candle in the container with no plant. Fire needs oxygen in order to burn. The candle in the container without a plant quickly uses up all the oxygen and goes out. The candle in the jar with the plant will burn for longer because the plant is constantly giving out oxygen through the process of photosynthesis.

At night plants do not give off as much oxygen as during the day because there is no Sun to power photosynthesis. If you repeated the activity in the dark, as suggested in the follow-up, you would probably have seen the candle in the container with the plant go out faster than it did in the light.

If you performed the follow-up activity with the pondweed, you may have noticed tiny bubbles of oxygen being released from the leaves. These bubbles drift up through the funnel and push the water out of the jar. Timing how fast the water goes down will give a good idea of how fast the plant is releasing oxygen.

The second follow-up demonstrates phototropism. Many people think that plants do not move. Plants do not move around in the same way as animals, but they do move. For example, as a plant grows, it slowly moves

The roots of a plant are very important because they allow water and other substances the plant needs to travel up to the stems and leaves.

toward light. This type of response is called a tropism. A plant's tropisms are controlled by chemicals, and the best known of them are called auxins. Auxins are made at the tips of growing roots and stems. They control the way the plant grows. Wherever a plant is growing, it will point its stems and leaves toward the light. That is called phototropism.

Phototropism happens because the auxins are produced wherever the light is coming from. If the light is shining directly down on top of a plant, the auxins spread out evenly and make the plant grow straight upward. If the light is coming from one side only, then the auxins build up on the sunny side of the stem. As a result, the cells on the shaded side of the stem grow longer, and the plant bends in the direction of the light.

Different plants store their food reserves in different places. The parts of plants that we eat are usually the parts containing the most of this stored food.

ACTIVITY 8
PURIFYING WATER

All life on Earth depends on water. For humans it is important that the water we use is clean because polluted water can cause diseases. Water taken from rivers and lakes or reused from the home must be treated first.

Humans, other animals, and plants all depend on water to survive. Every day the average person needs to drink several pints of water. Water is also needed for growing crops and for industry. It takes about 8,000 gallons (30,000 liters) of water to make a single car. Every time you take a shower, you use about 9 gallons (35 liters) of water.

Because we depend on water for so much, it is important that the water we use is free from pollutants that can harm us and the environment. Most chemicals dissolve in water; and while some, such as minerals, are useful to people, others can cause great harm. Bacteria and viruses that cause disease are also carried by water.

In water polluted with sewage and other waste bacteria have a lot to feed on and breed quickly. Many of these organisms are dangerous to human

● *Water contaminated with sewage is trickled over a gravel bed by a long rotating arm. The contaminated water is cleaned as it filters down through the gravel.*

health and cause diseases like cholera. Raw sewage has to be treated to remove these bacteria. Even today, in many parts of the world tens of thousands of people get sick every year from drinking or washing in water that has not been cleaned.

The process of cleaning water is called water purification. Water from rivers and lakes needs to be purified before it can be used, and water that has already been used must be cleaned for reuse.

When you flush a toilet, the sewage is carried to treatment plants by a network of underground pipes. There the waste flows through screens that filter out large objects. The sewage is then pumped through grit-removal channels, where small stones or sand sink to the bottom. This grit is washed to be used to fill holes in roads or on building sites.

The remaining sewage then passes into sedimentation tanks. Solid material settles to the bottom of these large tanks. This waste is called crude sludge. The crude sludge and the liquid above it then follow different routes. The liquid goes on to secondary treatment plants. There tiny organisms feed on any waste materials still left floating in the liquid. The organisms change the waste to harmless substances in about eight hours. The liquid left behind then goes to another sedimentation tank. There the valuable microorganisms are separated from the liquid so that they can be reused. The water that is left then flows into a river or can be further processed to be piped back into homes. In the United States chlorine is added to the water. It is a powerful chemical that helps kill bacteria.

The crude sludge is pumped into digestion tanks. In these tanks microorganisms feed on the waste for three to four weeks. As they do so, the organisms produce methane gas. This gas is sometimes used as fuel to power the sewage plant. As more water is removed from the sludge, it becomes a rich fertilizer that can be used by farmers.

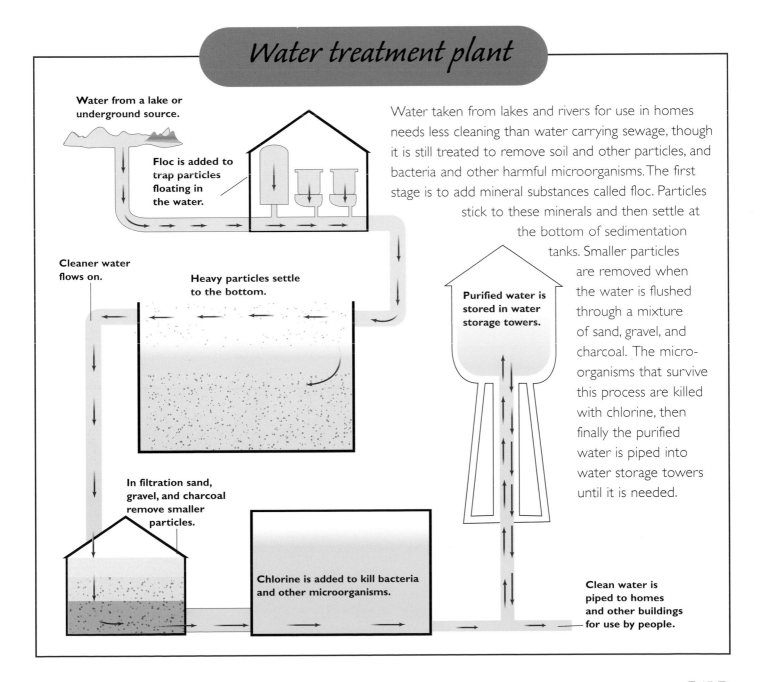

Water treatment plant

Water from a lake or underground source.

Floc is added to trap particles floating in the water.

Cleaner water flows on.

Heavy particles settle to the bottom.

In filtration sand, gravel, and charcoal remove smaller particles.

Chlorine is added to kill bacteria and other microorganisms.

Purified water is stored in water storage towers.

Clean water is piped to homes and other buildings for use by people.

Water taken from lakes and rivers for use in homes needs less cleaning than water carrying sewage, though it is still treated to remove soil and other particles, and bacteria and other harmful microorganisms. The first stage is to add mineral substances called floc. Particles stick to these minerals and then settle at the bottom of sedimentation tanks. Smaller particles are removed when the water is flushed through a mixture of sand, gravel, and charcoal. The microorganisms that survive this process are killed with chlorine, then finally the purified water is piped into water storage towers until it is needed.

Filtering Water

Goals

1. **Use different methods to purify water.**
2. **Demonstrate how water treatment works.**

What you will need:

- 3 jars
- pond water
- coffee filter
- cheesecloth
- sand
- gravel
- soil
- wire mesh
- funnel
- measuring cup

1 Pour some of the pond water into the measuring cup, and add "pollutants" to make the water as dirty as possible. Add watercolor paint, mud, and other dirty things to the water.

2 Place the coffee filter in the funnel, and set the funnel into one of the jars. Pour one-third of the dirty water through the filter, and let it soak through. When all the water has soaked through the filter, take the filter out, and place it to one side to dry.

Safety tip

Be careful when you collect the pond water. Make sure that the water is shallow, and don't stand too close to the edge. Wear rubber gloves, and scoop the water out with a bucket. Ask an adult to take you to the park if you don't have a pond in your yard.

3 Repeat step two with half the remaining dirty water, using another jar. This time, put a piece of cheesecloth in the funnel. Leave the cheesecloth filter to dry.

4 Place the funnel into the third jar. Place a piece of wire mesh on top of the funnel. Put a layer of gravel, about 1-inch (2.5cm) deep, on top of the mesh, then add a layer of sand and finally a layer of soil.

5 Pour the rest of the dirty water over the materials in the filter. Leave the water to soak through into the jar.

Troubleshooting

What if there was not much difference in the color of the water from the three filters?
Make sure that you are using really dirty water and that the wire mesh you use has small enough holes to prevent any of the sand and other solids from falling through and into the clean water.

6 Compare the water in all three jars and the solids left behind in the three filters. Which filter did the best job of purifying the water?

FOLLOW-UP   Filtering water

You can continue the activity using a variety of different filters. You may want to try using a paper towel or an old pillow case or t-shirt (be sure to ask permission first).

To demonstrate how solids settle out from a liquid, as in sewage treatment plants, mix up a jar of dirty water, and let it sit overnight. Any solids present will sink to the bottom, and the water will look much clearer than before.

Reed beds occur naturally in wetlands. They help control the flow of water in rivers and reduce flooding when rainfall is high. The reeds also act as natural water filters. Many water treatment plants use them in the purification process.

You can easily see how water is cleaned in reed beds by filling a jar with dirty or scummy pond water. Put some pondweed, water lily, or other water plant in the jar (right), and leave it in a sunny place. After a few days the water should start to look clearer as the water plant filters it. How long does it take for the water to become completely clear?

ANALYSIS
Purifying water

The three different types of filter you used in the experiment will each extract some of the dirt from the water but not all of it. How much they extract depends on the type of filter and cheesecloth you used. The larger the holes, the less solids they will filter out. This type of filter will mainly remove solids, but not anything that is dissolved in the water. Sand and gravel filters, like the third filter you made, are used to clean water in systems that also use reed beds.

Reed beds are a natural way to clean up rivers and water systems. Water flows through the reed beds, and as it flows, solids such as dirt and soil are caught by the plants. In this way the plants act as a natural filter. The plants also use organic waste (sewage) in the water as food. The reed beds themselves are a habitat for a wide range of creatures, including frogs, toads, newts, and many birds.

Reeds and water plants are very good at filtering sewage because much of the dirt and waste in sewage is high in nitrogen. It is a very important element and is necessary for life. Plants use the nitrogen from waste in order to grow better (see box on next page).

In the world's tropical regions, where the temperature is high, bacteria cause the soil to lose its nitrogen. This means that the soil is poor quality and that plants could remove all the nitrogen very quickly. Rice paddy fields solve this problem. The waterlogged soil slows down the actions of the bacteria and thereby keeps the nitrogen in. Flooded fields are also good for the growth of blue-green algae (cyanobacteria), which change nitrogen from the atmosphere into nitrogen compounds.

Farmers add nitrogen fertilizers to the soil to increase the amount of food that they grow. But there is now worry that farmers may be over-loading the system with nitrogen. The nitrates that they add to the soil often seep out of the soil before they can be used by the crops. They then enter rivers and other sources of water. Too much nitrogen can cause plant and algal overgrowth, which can be damaging for human health. In some parts of the world water for domestic use has such high levels of nitrogen that it is unsafe to drink.

■ *Water plants benefit from the nitrogen that leaks out of the soil into water. However, too much can lead to overgrowth, and rivers can become choked.*

Nitrogen cycle

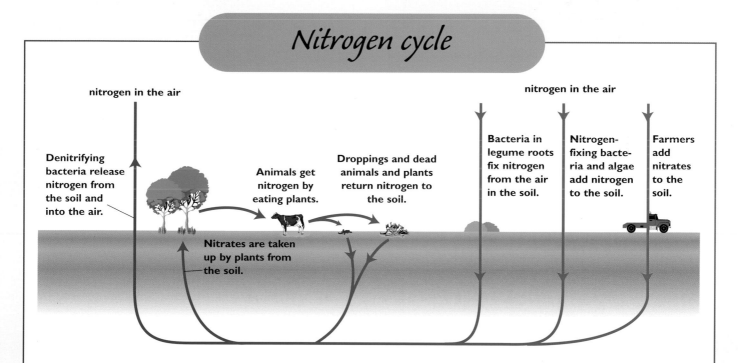

nitrogen in the air

nitrogen in the air

Denitrifying bacteria release nitrogen from the soil and into the air.

Animals get nitrogen by eating plants.

Droppings and dead animals and plants return nitrogen to the soil.

Bacteria in legume roots fix nitrogen from the air in the soil.

Nitrogen-fixing bacteria and algae add nitrogen to the soil.

Farmers add nitrates to the soil.

Nitrates are taken up by plants from the soil.

Nitrogen makes up 78 percent of air, but it cannot be used by animals or plants while it is a gas. Nitrogen in the air is changed by lightning into nitrogen dioxide. It combines with drops of rain to fall to the ground as nitric acid. Nitrogen is also converted into usable compounds by nitrogen-fixing bacteria and plants such as lichen and algae. They change it into chemicals called nitrates. The nitrates are a form of nitrogen that can be taken up by the roots of plants. The plants are then eaten by animals in turn. Some nitrogen is passed out in manure. This manure and animal remains then help feed the soil. This is called the nitrogen cycle.

ACTIVITY 9
DECOMPOSITION

Garbage is simply anything that you don't want. That doesn't mean it's not useful. To some insects, bacteria, and fungi natural waste is food, and it forms a necessary part of their life cycle.

Any waste in an ecosystem is called detritus. It includes dead organisms and animal droppings. The natural world disposes of waste by breaking it down and reusing it. There are some animals that only feed off this detritus. They are called detritovores, or decomposers, and include dung beetles, millipedes, slugs and snails, springtails, wood lice, and worms. These animals eat larger pieces of detritus and turn it into smaller waste droppings. These droppings can be more easily digested by smaller decomposers such as bacteria and fungi, which then break the waste down to basic chemicals. As they carry out this important task, they release carbon dioxide, which is used by plants. Almost all the material an organism takes in during its lifetime returns to the earth as waste.

● *A dung beetle moves many times its own weight in dung every year. Adults eat some of the dung, and some is buried for the beetle's larvae (offspring) to eat.*

Some substances take longer to break down. Plants, for example, contain a substance called cellulose in their twigs, leaves, and stems. It is a very tough material that protects and supports the plant. Very few organisms can break down cellulose. Bacteria and fungi are the main decomposers of cellulose. If you visit a forest or a wooded area, you will find dead branches lying on the ground. Some of them will have fungi growing on them. Others may crumble at a touch. That is because bacteria are slowly doing their work and breaking down the cellulose.

Humans produce a lot of waste, and much of it cannot be broken down by decomposers and therefore takes up more and more space. Without decomposers it takes materials like plastics and metals a very long time to break down. When waste is buried, it is called landfill. Landfill is the cheapest way to get rid of garbage; but as the amount of trash we produce increases, landfill sites become fuller. Also, as the natural materials in the landfill break down, chemicals that are produced by this process seep into the soil. This seepage is called leechate.

An alternative to landfills is to burn the garbage. Burning garbage reduces its volume, but the ash that is produced contains poisonous chemicals that pollute the atmosphere and can make people sick.

In the activity on the following pages you will have an opportunity to experiment with the rates of decay of different substances.

Fungi, such as these mushrooms, are very important decomposers. As they feed on dead matter and droppings, they release nutrients that other organisms, such as bacteria and plants, use.

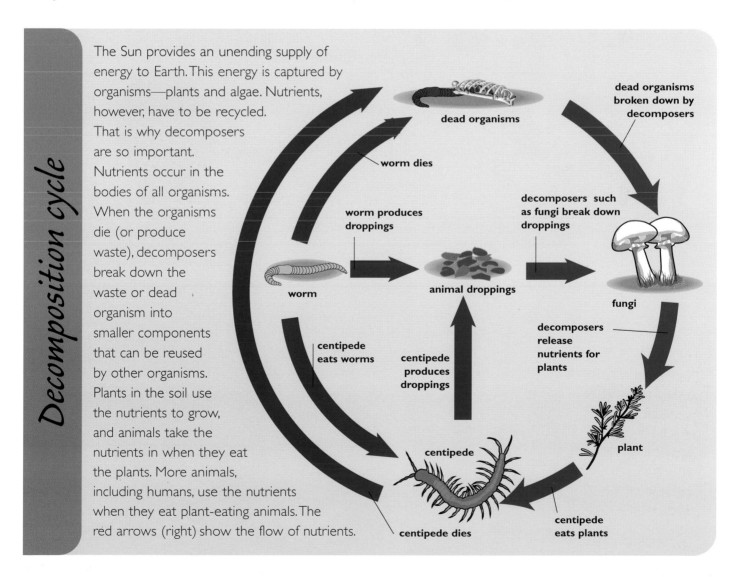

Decomposition cycle

The Sun provides an unending supply of energy to Earth. This energy is captured by organisms—plants and algae. Nutrients, however, have to be recycled. That is why decomposers are so important. Nutrients occur in the bodies of all organisms. When the organisms die (or produce waste), decomposers break down the waste or dead organism into smaller components that can be reused by other organisms. Plants in the soil use the nutrients to grow, and animals take the nutrients in when they eat the plants. More animals, including humans, use the nutrients when they eat plant-eating animals. The red arrows (right) show the flow of nutrients.

dead organisms

worm dies

worm produces droppings

dead organisms broken down by decomposers

decomposers such as fungi break down droppings

worm

animal droppings

fungi

centipede eats worms

centipede produces droppings

decomposers release nutrients for plants

centipede

plant

centipede dies

centipede eats plants

Rate of Decay

Goals

1. **Compare different rates of decay.**
2. **Determine which materials best prevent or slow decay.**

What you will need:

- *three slices of white bread*
- *paintbrush*
- *water-based paint*
- *spray bottle filled with water*
- *empty spray bottle*
- *three plastic plates*
- *pen for labeling the plates*
- *bleach*

1 Using the pen, label one plate "water," label the second plate "bleach–water," and label the third plate "paint."

Too much trash

Each week the average American household produces 54 pounds (24kg) of solid waste. In a single year the average person in New York City throws away eight or nine times their own body weight in trash.

2 Place one slice of bread on each plate.

3 Ask an adult to mix a few tablespoons of bleach with a cup of plain water in a spray-bottle. Spray this mixture onto the bread on the "bleach-water" plate.

What if none of the slices of bread turn moldy?

If it is warm and dry, the bread may dry out, which makes it hard for mold to grow. You can keep this from happening by spraying the bread every day to keep it moist. Make sure you always spray the "water" bread with plain water and the "bleach–water" bread with your bleach–water solution.

4 Spray the bread on the "water" plate with plain water.

Safety tip

Make sure you leave the bread in a place where bugs or rats will not be attracted to them. Once mold has started to grow on the bread, handle them only while wearing gloves.

5 Use the paintbrush to paint the last slice of bread. Now leave all three slices out in your house. Which slice decays first? Which slice develops the most mold? It may take several days or weeks for mold to grow.

▶ *After a week or so, mold will start to grow on your bread. The bread that has been treated with the most chemicals will decay (mold) at the slowest rate.*

FOLLOW-UP

Rate of decay

A quarter of the contents of the average garbage can is food waste. Most of it can be recycled into compost, along with garden waste. Compost can then be used on flower beds to improve the soil.

You can make a simple compost pile using just a bucket. This type of compost pile has no ventilation and so is called an anaerobic (without air) digester.

Ask an adult to cut the bottom out of an old bucket. Push the bucket into the ground, then fill it with kitchen and garden waste. Add a tin can and a plastic bag, and mix it all up together. Cover the food waste with dirt. To speed the composting, cover the bucket with a piece of old carpet. As the bacteria start to work, the material in the bucket will begin to heat up.

Plant some plants around the bucket. Do they grow better or faster than plants farther away from the compost?

After one to two months the waste will all be broken down. Remove the compost from the bucket, and use it as fertilizer.

ANALYSIS

Decomposition

Organisms like mold (a type of fungi) and bacteria eat and break down natural materials. You cannot always see these organisms, but you can see their work whenever you look at a rotten piece of food. Natural substances, like food, break down much faster than artificial substances, like plastic and chemicals, because bacteria and mold are able to eat natural substances.

In this activity you treated three identical slices of bread in three different ways. Bleach kills bacteria and mold, which is why it is used as a disinfectant around the house, so you should not have seen much mold on the bread treated with the bleach-water. Paint is also made from chemicals that kill mold and bacteria. The coating of paint should have done a very good job of keeping mold and bacteria from eating the bread.

Most types of mold and bacteria prefer to live in a warm, moist environment. The bread sprayed with plain water provides such an environment and should have been covered with mold in a week or so.

Processed and sliced white bread, like the kind we used here, contains chemicals that prevent the bread from molding. If you try the activity again with organic or homemade bread, you will probably find that it molds much more quickly.

In the follow-up activity you had the chance to build a small compost pile. A compost pile is a great way to recycle food waste. Keeping the food in an enclosed space speeds up decomposition and reduces the smell. If you are not squeamish, you could look at your compost heap from time to time while it decomposes (do not touch it at any time). After a few weeks the food will not be recognizable any more. And after one or two months (depending on the time of year) decomposers will have broken down the food waste into a mixture resembling dark soil. It is compost, and it is rich with nutrients

● *Because cans do not decompose quickly in the absence of air, they can be recycled as building materials.*

that help plants grow. You may want to use it as potting soil or fertilizer. Inside your compost you will find the plastic bag and tin can. They will not have broken down.

If you want to help cut down on the amount of waste that is created, you need to use fewer things that do not decompose. Reduce the number of items you buy that have plastic packaging, and use only as many chemicals, like paint and bleach, as you absolutely need to. Before you throw anything away, try to reuse or recycle it. And build a compost pile in your yard or garden to allow decomposers to get rid of waste for you.

▼ *This huge landfill site in Hong Kong is needed to accommodate the garbage produced by the island.*

ACTIVITY 10
BIOSPHERE

All life on Earth shares the same biosphere—the part of the planet capable of supporting life. Everything living in a part of the biosphere contributes in some way to the health of the whole planet.

The biosphere is the part of the planet that can support life. It stretches to the depths of the oceans, a few hundred meters below land, and to a height of more than 20,000 feet (6,000m). Everything within this capsule, living and nonliving, is part of the biosphere. Thus the biosphere includes not only plants and animals, but also minerals, soils, water, atmosphere, and even sunlight. All of these different components are constantly changing and interacting with each other.

Within Earth's biosphere are a huge variety of different ecosystems and habitats. Although organisms share their habitat with other plants and animals, all the organisms within each habitat have different behaviors, activities, and feeding patterns. The way an organism fits into and uses the different parts of its habitat is called its niche.

All organisms have adaptations. They can be physical traits or ways of behaving that help the organism make the best use of their habitat. Organisms that seem to be competing with each other can actually coexist in the same ecosystem if they ocupy different niches. For example, two barnacle species, *Balanus* and *Chthalamus*, occupy the same shoreline and use the same food resources. However, *Balanus* occupies the lower shore, while *Chthalamus* survives well on the upper shore because of its greater ability to resist drying out at low tide.

All organisms depend on each other in some way. For example, different types of organisms (species) sometimes share parts of their niches. Mutualisms are relationships in which two organisms benefit from living together. For example, lichen consists of a fungus and an algae growing together. Both organisms benefit from this arrangement. The algae makes food, which the fungus also uses, through photosynthesis, while the fungus protects the algae and stores water for both.

🔵 **This artificial biosphere in Arizona is a closed system—nothing gets in except for sunlight. It was built to study ways of colonizing other planets.**

■ *Several different species of animals can share the same habitat or environment, but each organism has its own ecological niche within its community.*

Not all close relationships are good for both sides. Some plants and animals, called parasites, live on or in another organism. They take food from a host organism and give nothing in return. A parasite rarely kills its host because that would cause its own death. Lice and fleas are parasites. Humans can be affected by parasites like tapeworms and roundworms.

Groups of animals of the same species sometimes live together in a colony. Many seabirds form colonies because there is safety in larger numbers. Ants, termites, and bees live in complex colonies. Different individuals perform specific roles on which the whole colony depends. Without worker bees, for example, or the queen bee the whole bee colony would collapse.

To survive, all organisms depend on their relationships with other organisms and with the nonliving parts of their environment. These relationships are often in delicate balance. If something happens to upset the balance, many organisms can be affected. For example, if one type of plant becomes extinct, then insects and small animals that rely on that plant for food could also die, as could birds that build nests using that plant and larger animals that eat the smaller animals.

The following activity lets you explore the relationship between living and nonliving parts of a habitat by building a miniature biosphere.

Food chains

In all environments organisms form food chains in which each organism preys (eats) on others and is in turn preyed on (eaten). Food chains interconnect to form food webs. The illustration below is a simplified version of a food web. The arrows show the direction of nutrient flow. For example, cats eat small birds, so the arrow shows that the nutrients move from the bird (prey) to the cat (predator).

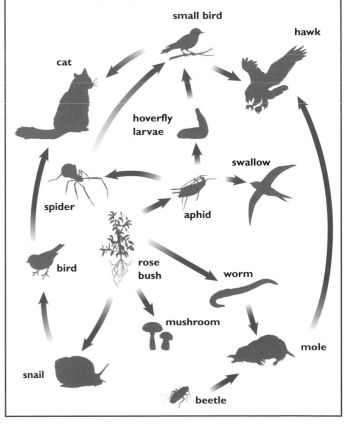

Biosphere in a Bottle

Goals

1. **Create a mini-biosphere.**
2. **Observe ways in which different organisms interact.**

What you will need:

- *clean quart jar (Mason jar) with a screw-top lid*
- *wax*
- *pond or lake water*
- *mud from a pond or lake*
- *water plants from an aquarium (such as* Elodea)
- *water snails*

1 Ask an adult to make a hole in the lid with a nail. Cover the hole with a small piece of wax. It will act as a valve to release gases that might build up inside the jar.

2 Fill the jar ⅔ to ¾ full with pond water.

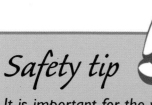

Safety tip

It is important for the wax valve to be put in the lid because a buildup of carbon dioxide gas could make the biosphere explode.

3 Add ½ to 1½ inches (1–4cm) of mud from the pond bottom. Don't worry if the water looks mucky—the mud will settle at the bottom.

4 Add some *Elodea* or other small water plants.

5 Add some larger water plants and small pond-living creatures, such as snails. Do not add larger animals.

6 Put the lid on the jar, and make careful observations of the contents over the next few weeks. Record the color of the water and the amount of light passing through, using descriptions such as sunny, overcast, or shady.

7 Watch over the next few weeks to see what happens in your biosphere, recording any changes that take place. After you are finished making observations, empty the contents of your biosphere into a nearby pond.

Reproduction

Every organism has a different way of reproducing. The simplest single-celled creatures, amebas, reproduce by splitting into two. Plants produce seeds that fall to the ground, produce roots and stalks, and start to grow. Birds, fish, snails, and reptiles reproduce by laying eggs. Insects lay eggs that hatch into grubs (larvae), such as caterpillars or maggots. Caterpillars turn into chrysalises (other larvae form pupae) and then into the adult insect. Mammals reproduce by giving birth to a baby, which drinks its mother's milk.

FOLLOW-UP Biosphere in a bottle

Record what you see by drawing a picture or taking photographs of the biosphere. You can repeat the experiment with smaller jars and carry out tests to see what happens if the environment changes because of pollution or other causes. It is important that we have respect for the natural world, and that the minimum amount of harm and damage is done to plants and creatures in these experiments.

Once your biosphere is established, after a couple of weeks you can remove some of the water and put it into a smaller jar. What effect does the smaller environment have on the creatures and plants inside the smaller biosphere?

You could also construct a larger biosphere. Conduct research on the types of plants and animals that live in certain environments. Can you design a biosphere that will duplicate those conditions?

If you notice that the plants and animals in your biosphere are not very healthy, you may decide to stop your experiment and release all the creatures back to the wild. If this happens, think about why the biosphere could not support life—what was missing? If this happens, it is not a failure. You can learn just as much this way as you can if your biosphere lasts for months.

You can make biospheres in several different sizes, but there will probably be an optimum (best) size of environment for the varieties of plants and animals that you use.

ANALYSIS
Biosphere

As time passes, you should notice changes taking place in the biosphere. The water will become clearer as the plants take up nutrients in the water, and creatures that may have been eggs in the mud at the beginning of the experiment will start to hatch and populate the habitat. Although you should keep your habitat closed, you can open it briefly to remove a small amount of water for closer observation.

Watch for patterns of feeding that may be taking place within the biosphere. How many of the creatures are plant eaters (herbivores), and how many eat other creatures (carnivores)? There must always be a balance in the number and type of organisms in any environment.

This delicate balance is constantly under threat of change. If one organism starts to reproduce more than others, then the balance is changed, and the food chains in the environment will also be altered. If the population of predators (animals that feed on other animals) is reduced, then prey animals will thrive. This can have a devastating effect on the whole ecosystem. Some of these effects are natural changes caused by weather patterns, for example, but many environmental changes are caused by human activities.

■ *Ecosystems are finely balanced systems of living and nonliving parts of Earth. Destroying a hedgerow results in the death of large numbers of plants and animals.*

Before Europeans arrived in Australia, the native plants and animals lived in balance. In 1859 a settler from England imported 24 pairs of rabbits into Australia. Since rabbits had never existed in Australia, there were no predators or parasites that ate rabbits. By 1889, without any predators to eat them, the rabbit population had grown to more than 24 million. The rabbits ate the natural vegetation, destroying the food of native animals, and turning once fertile areas of landscape into dry desert.

Many habitats have also been removed, which kills off plants and animals. In Britain hedgerows that divided the fields once contained many species of plants and animals. As farms and fields became bigger, many hedgerows were removed, the organisms that lived in them had nowhere to find their food, and they, too, died out.

Feeding off others

All organisms need to eat. Plants are producers—they use the Sun's energy to produce food so they can live and grow. Plants are then eaten by animals (herbivores) called primary consumers. Animals that eat other animals are called secondary consumers (carnivores). Other animals, called tertiary consumers, eat the secondary consumers. The links between different animals and plants and how they eat is called a food chain. Each food chain also contains decomposers, such as bacteria, fungi, and some insects, which obtain their energy by breaking down dead plant and animal material. An ecosystem contains many different food chains, which link to form a complex food web. That is because most animals eat a variety of things and so take part in a number of food chains. For example, the birds in this photo (right) eat the lice and bugs (parasites) that feed on the buffalo's blood. The buffalo tolerates the birds because they help rid it of annoying parasites. Without the birds the buffalo would suffer from parasites, and without the buffalo the birds would go hungry.

GLOSSARY

acid rain: Polluted rain, snow, or mist.

anaerobic: Without oxygen.

atmosphere: The layer of gas that surrounds a planet. Earth's atmosphere is also called the air.

atom: The smallest particle in an element that still has the chemical properties of that element.

auxin: A chemical that directs a plant's growth.

biodegradable: Anything, including a few plastics, that can be broken down by microscopic organisms.

biome: All the ecosystems that share the same geographical region and climate.

biosphere: The part of the planet that supports life.

carbohydrates: Compounds built by plants from water and carbon dioxide by the process of photosynthesis.

carnivore: Any creature that feeds largely on meat.

cellulose: A tough material that forms the walls of plant cells and supports the plant.

chlorophyll: A green substance in plant leaves and algae that traps sunlight to power photosynthesis.

chloroplasts: Microscopic structures in leaves that contain chlorophyll.

colony: A large number of animals of the same species living together as a group.

community: A habitat in which different populations of organisms all live together.

compound: A substance made of atoms of more than one element. The smallest unit of a compound is called a molecule.

corrosion: A chemical reaction in which acids eat away materials.

cyanobacteria: Bacteria (or blue-green algae) that change nitrogen in the atmosphere into nitrogen compounds.

decomposition: A process in which organic matter is broken down into its chemical parts.

ecosystem: Several different communities of organisms and the physical area in which they live.

electron: An extremely small particle that orbits the nucleus (center) of an atom. Electrons have a negative electric charge.

element: A substance that cannot be broken down into even simpler substances by chemical reactions. An element contains only one kind of atom.

emissions: Substances, such as smoke and fumes, given off into the air.

environment: The combined physical and biological conditions that influence an organism's life.

food chain: A series of different living organisms, each one of which feeds on one or more organisms down the chain.

food web: Different food chains linked together.

fossil fuel: A type of fuel, such as coal, oil, or natural gas, formed deep in the Earth by the decomposition of plants or animals.

global warming: The increase in the temperature of the atmosphere as the greenhouse effect increases.

glucose: A type of sugar produced by plants.

greenhouse gas: A gas, such as carbon dioxide, that traps heat from the Sun in the atmosphere.

greenhouse effect: The way that the Earth's atmosphere traps the Sun's heat.

habitat: The type of place where an organism can live.

herbivore: Any creature that feeds on plants.

humus: A rich soil produced when dead organisms break down and combine with minerals in the soil.

individual: Any single living organism.

landfill: A site where people bury solid waste.

mold: A type of fungus.

mutualism: A relationship in which two organisms benefit from living together.

niche: An organism's role in its ecosystem, defined by what it feeds on, its habitat, and other relationships.

nitrogen cycle: The continuous circulation of nitrogen from the air to the ground (in nitrogen-fixing bacteria), into plants and then into animals, and back into the ground through waste products and death.

nucleus: The center of an atom.

ozone: A naturally occurring colorless gas.

ozone layer: A layer of gas high in the atmosphere that absorbs most of the radiation from the Sun that can damage living organisms.

palisade cells: Layer of cells that contains chloroplasts, immediately beneath the outer surface of a plant leaf.

parasite: Any plant or animal that lives on or in another organism.

photosynthesis: The process by which plants use sunlight to turn carbon dioxide and water into sugars for food.

phototropism: The movement and growth of a plant toward light.

pollution: Contamination of an area—land, air, or water—with unnatural substances or an excess of a natural one, usually through human activity.

population: A group of organisms of the same species all living in the same place.

predator: Any animal that kills other animals for food.

primary consumers: Animals that eat plants.

respiration: The process by which living organisms release energy from food.

secondary consumers: Animals that eat plant-eating animals, which are also called primary consumers.

soil erosion: Loss of the top layer or layers of soil, worn away by water or by wind.

species: Related organisms that form a distinct type, that look like one another, and are able to breed within that type but not with organisms of other species.

starch: Natural compounds that are made up of complex carbohydrates. Plants store carbohydrates as starches.

symbiosis: A relationship in which two organisms live together, often to their mutual benefit.

tertiary consumers: Animals that eat animals that are secondary consumers.

tropism: The response of a plant to an outside change.

zooplankton: Microscopic animals that live in water.

SET INDEX

Page numbers in *italics* refer to pictures or their captions. **Bold** numbers refer to volume number.